I Will Not Be Afraid

By Michelle Medlock Adams

Illustrated by Jeremy Tugeau

CONCORDIA PUBLISHING HOUSE • SAINT LOUIS

When the thunder booms—KABOOM!
and when the lightning strikes,
I will not be afraid at all!
I won't yell, "EEK!" or "YIKES!"

For my brother, Rob,
the bravest big brother a girl ever had.
I love you!

Your kid sister,
Michelle "Missy" Medlock Adams

For Memom and Popup

J.T.

Published 2008 by Concordia Publishing House
3558 S. Jefferson Avenue
St. Louis, MO 63118-3968
1-800-325-3040 • www.cph.org

Manufactured in China

1 2 3 4 5 6 7 8 9 10   17 16 15 14 13 12 11 10 09 08

And when it's really dark at night
and I'm alone in bed,
I will not be afraid at all!
I will not hide my head.

❖ You are my hiding place; You will
protect me from trouble and surround
me with songs of deliverance.
Psalm 32:7

And when I meet new boys and girls

and I am feeling shy,

I will not be afraid at all.

I will not scream or cry.

❖ Therefore do not worry.
Matthew 6:34

And when I have to go on stage

to sing my special part,

I will not be afraid at all!

I'll sing with all my heart!

❖ Sing joyfully to the LORD,
you righteous; it is fitting
for the upright to praise Him.
Psalm 33:1

And if our country is at war
and trouble's everywhere,
I will not be afraid at all
'cause I know God is there.

✤ God has said, "Never will I leave
you; never will I forsake you." So we
say with confidence, "The Lord is my
helper; I will not be afraid."
Hebrews 13:5–6

I do not have to be afraid
     when bad things come my way.
I will not be afraid at all!
     That's what I have to say!

My God is in control of all—
     the storms, the night, the war.
I trust God and love Him so.
     He loves me even more!

❖ Cast all your anxiety on Him
because He cares for you.
1 Peter 5:7

God is bigger than anything,
lots bigger than my fears,
And I can call on Him for help,
'cause when I pray, He hears!

✤ "Because he loves Me," says the Lord,
"I will rescue him; I will protect him, for he
acknowledges My name. He will call upon
Me, and I will answer him; I will be with him
in trouble, I will deliver him and honor him."
Psalm 91:14–15

God made me to be brave and strong.

But even when I'm not,

God helps me not to be afraid

'cause He loves me a lot!

❖ I can do everything through
Him who gives me strength.
Philippians 4:13

God promises to never leave.

He's always here with me.

That's why I will not be afraid.

I have no need to be!

✤ For He will command
His angels concerning you
to guard you in all your ways.
Psalm 91:11

God sent His Son to die for me.
That sure is great to know!
'Cause even when my life is through,
I know just where I'll go.

I'll go to heaven up above—
and there's no fear up there.
I'll live forever with my Lord,
forever in His care.

❖ For God did not give us a spirit
of timidity, but a spirit of power,
of love and of self-discipline.
2 Timothy 1:7

'Til then I'll say, "Lord, take my sins,
protect me every day.
Thank You so much for loving me
and hearing when I pray!

"I will not be afraid at all
because You are my Friend.
Your perfect love removes my fear,
and Your love has no end."

❖ Have I not commanded you? Be strong
and courageous. Do not be terrified; do not
be discouraged, for the LORD your God will
be with you wherever you go.
Joshua 1:9

PARENTING MOMENT

The Bible says we do not have a spirit of fear, so do not be afraid! The Bible also tells us that God will never leave us, so we are never alone! Isn't that good to know? Talk with your child about fears of all kinds and about ways to combat those fears. Together, write a prayer that will help to alleviate these fears and instill confidence in the protection and promises that are ours through Christ. This prayer can be as simple as:

"Jesus, I know You are here with me, and I will not be afraid."

Then, the next time something happens to frighten your child, you can remind him that he is always in God's care and grace.